YOU, RESOURCEFUL

Return To Who You Want To Be

by

Kristin Prevallet

—————

wide reality books

You, Resourceful: Return To Who You Want To Be

2nd edition.
Kindle version: *You, Resourceful: Tap Your Inner Resources to Restore Your Mind and Body*

Bio photo: Richard Ryan

for Richard and Sophie

and

for everyone who believes that
internal changes create external
shifts — one person at a time.

TABLE OF CONTENTS

Unlike some writers of self-help books, I don't think that the goal of self-awareness is to eliminate stress from your life. Nor is it to work out a deal with the universe that will shield you from ever having anything bad happen.

With that in mind, I've written this book to reassure you that stress is inevitable, that you will encounter mean people, and that your life will carry on in spite of many moments of sadness and exhaustion.

But the reality of stress, suffering, disappointment, and impermanence doesn't have to break you.

And your reactions to these things don't have to destroy your body.

This book is a synthesis of ideas that many other writers have been writing about for a long time; it is a convergence of knowledge that has been passed down in alternative healing practices and poetic texts for thousands of years. Take it and process it in your own way. And then pass it on.

YOU, REVOLVING

Wrapped in your down bag
Starlight on your cheeks and eyelids
Your breath comes and goes
In a tiny cloud in the frosty night.
Ten thousand birds sing in the sunrise.
Ten thousand years revolve without change.
All this will never be again.

-from "The Wheel Revolves" by Kenneth Rexroth

What does your life revolve around? It's an expression to be curious about. *A revolving* is a turning of celestial bodies (planets around a sun, moons around a planet). The word eventually evolved to mean "revolution" in the sense of *to turn, to roll back* — as in a great systemic change.

It's interesting that when people say:

"my life revolves around _____"

they usually fill in the blank with something they do habitually that should feel good, but ultimately stresses them out. A Google search of "My life revolves around _____" revealed habits that make people feel out of control such as:

My life revolves around my boyfriend. HELP!
My whole life revolves around food.
My whole life revolves around drugs.
My social life revolves around alcohol.
My life revolves around video games.
My life revolves around marijuana, should I quit?

The phrase "my life revolves around _____" seems to convey a force outside of us, as if we are acting out our lives in response to the gravitational pull of circumstance.

Some people describe this idea of revolving as the feeling of being out of control, like a gerbil in an exercise wheel that is trapped in a cage. Or, they will explain how they are repeating patterns and behaviors over and over again without knowing why. Some people will say that these patterns feel like blocks, or walls that they just can't break down or move beyond no matter how hard they try.

Perhaps this is because they're complaining to the wrong department. It doesn't do much good to file a grievance with the crossing guard if you're upset about the education system. She might be sympathetic to your plight, but you certainly can't expect her to go out of her way to contact the Board of Ed. It's not her job, and the more you badger her, the more annoyed she's going to get. She's in charge of focusing on the flow of passers-by and traffic—why would you expect her to be in charge of the entire system?

My life revolves, like string around a spool and moons around a planet. I rotate, turn, spin, wheel, gyrate, circle, whirl around…

…and if that revolving isn't making you feel good, what would you like your life to revolve around instead? If you could put your foot on the ground, stop the merry-go-round and with all your might push it in the opposite direction, what would you like to have happen?

As at the far edge of circling the country
facing suddenly the other ocean,
the boundless edge of what I had wanted
to know, I stepped
    into my answers' shadow ocean

....

-from "As at the Far Edge of Circling" by Ed
Roberson

Aw, Snap!

You may think your life revolves around (*fill in the blank*) but unwanted addictions, symptoms, patterns, and behaviors are often the outward manifestations of internal responses to stress. Tremors on the surface of a planet may steal our attention, but the underlying trigger is a complex convergence of external conditions including solar flares and atmospheric pressure, as well as the internal movement of plates and fault lines below the surface. In other words, sometimes it's important to pay attention to all that is happening behind the scenes of the symptom.

I've read over and over again that many doctors believe that the majority of symptoms their patients experience are related to stress. But this doesn't mean that stress is always negative. When you're finishing up a proposal for work, driving your injured friend to the emergency room, calling (or out-running) the police, or rushing to make it on time to work, the abundance of cortisol and adrenaline is a performance enhancer. It gives you a terrific jolt and a sense of urgency that is essential to feeling productive and filled with purpose.

But if your life revolves around stress, your body is stuck in a state of constant alarm and like any good fire station, it will respond with a surge of hormones, including adrenaline and cortisol. And if the blaze can't be quelled and continues to rage, those hormones will continue to surge. This will cause your vital organs to operate on overdrive, disrupting almost all of your body's natural self-regulating processes. This means that your immune system will trigger inflammation and your brain will trigger feelings of fear and panic. And as you can imagine, this will ignite a vicious cycle.

Let's say that you have just absentmindedly left your computer bag on the subway. The first thought you have (probably something like "I am such an idiot!!) will set off a cascade of reactions firing through your entire system so quickly that by the time you fill up with a red hot fury and curse the universe, the thought that triggered the reactions will be long gone.

All that will be left is your body, seething with rage, now fueled with cortisol and adrenaline, searching for the appropriate response. This response might be to run after the train as fast as you can and then jump onto it like Spiderman, flinging yourself on board. But if this doesn't work, what good are all those stress hormones a little while later when you're on the phone with lost-and-found, snapping and snarling at the person on the other end of the line?

Even though losing your computer bag is a major setback, unless you're carrying a top secret microchip and are being pursued by the mob, it's probably not a life or death situation. If you're still freaked out about it hours later, you're remaining in fight-or-flight mode for way too long. As if this setback, this incredible annoyance, this major inconvenience deserves the same response as that bus speeding towards you or that pit bull charging at your poodle's jugular.

Rationally you know that there is no parallel; that compared to other events when you could really use that hormonal response, losing your bag is a blip on the timeline of your life. But unless you convince your body and mind that you're safe, in control, and capable of dealing with the situation you're probably going to trigger a self-deprecating spiral that could last for days.

What a weird species we are. Can you imagine a wolf, pissed off that a rabbit outran him, carrying around his anger for the rest of the day? So distracted by his emotions that he lunges and attacks everything in his path? He'd be dead by noon.

Why do humans carry around so much emotional spill-over? It must have something to do with our survival (even though it also seems to contribute to our tendencies towards self-destruction). I don't have all the answers but I do know that holding on to emotions long after the initial trigger entails throwing logs onto a fire that has been rekindled on and off for many years.

This is because like a current sweeping everything into its path, there is a part of your brain that actively gathers and retains your sensory and emotional experiences of the world. What is swept up isn't necessarily "memories" in the sense of coherent images or scenes that replay in your mind; it's more like a storage of reactions that are emotional, auditory, sensory, and kinesthetic. They're cellular, muscular, and circulatory. They are life at every stage of living, whether you remember or you don't.

In their book *Power Up Your Brain: The Neuroscience of Enlightenment,* David Perlmutter and Alberto Villoldo call this an "instinctual memory." They discuss how this memory is connected to the "ancient survival instinct" part of our brain, centralized in the limbic system. In other words, there is no real reason why you carry around the lingering feelings of something that happened to you hours earlier, except that the incident triggered something much deeper in your limbic brain that confused a momentary disturbance with an actual threat of danger.

They write:

"Many of life's typical events are inappropriately routed through the limbic brain where we relive—

from an emotional perspective—the trauma that may have occurred decades ago. The limbic brain can't distinguish between a painful event that occurred twenty years ago and the memory of that event triggered by a similar situation today."

This sounds as if your limbic brain is separate from "you." It's not, except that it sure can seem that way when you are reacting to things in a way that makes you feel out of control.

It's unlikely that you will remember the exact scenes and specific incidents in your life when your body first reacted to mental events in a physical manner. But you can be assured that whenever you encounter (or even just think about) something that threatens you, this part of your brain will put your vitals into overdrive and surge hormones through your nervous system to meet the situation head-on, or to quickly flee if you can't handle the situation.

As you continue on your journey of self-awareness and healing it's important to remember that your body's stress-response system is self-regulating. Once a perceived threat has passed, hormone levels drop so that your body can return to a coherent, functional state. Your heart rate and blood pressure return to baseline levels, and your organs resume their life-preserving functions.

Of course, returning to calm after experiencing a flood of stress hormones isn't always easy or pleasant. Luckily your body and mind *want* to reveal your inner resources and help you to calmly deal with the situation.

The computer and the bag are gone. How long are you going to carry them around?

Neighbor

everyday

you get up

coughing

harking

screaming at the dog

cursing yourself out

& for what

you are there

you see something coming

the event happens

and you can't go back to the beginning

- "Neighbor" by Jayne Cortez

YOUR MIND IS A MULTIPLEX CINEMA

Although there are many definitions, think of this behind-the-scenes limbic brain and the physiological reactions it triggers as "the unconscious mind." Because when it comes to understanding the mindbody connection, it's important to remember that any change you want to make needs to fit in with the beliefs, values, ways of thinking, and past experience for which you've already laid the groundwork. Declaring "I will not over-react no matter what" is going to fall on deaf ears if your limbic brain and the physiological responses it triggers associate absent-mindedly losing things with being out of control —a feeling most people unconsciously associate as a threat to their survival. This means that in the split second when you realize you have lost something important, your unconscious mind is going to forget about your intention to "not over-react" because it conflicts with what you, in some deeply held belief, feel to be true about your sense of self and survival. This includes what you feel you are capable of, given your past experiences, and your track record for making similar changes.

So how do you go about talking to this mind of yours, the one that doesn't respond when it is bossed around or is expected to diverge from its habits? It might be helpful to imagine your well-meaning but sometimes conflicted unconscious mind as an entity who enjoys telling and hearing stories, parables and metaphors. And it might be good to know that the stories you tell yourself (about who you are, where you came from, what you're capable of, and what you're not) all come from this entity. So if you don't think that your unconscious mind's interpretation of those stories is useful to you anymore, you can begin telling some different ones. That will at least get its attention.

Then I placed
my mask on a stone, and walked as the sleepless
walk, led by my dream. And from one moon
to another I leapt. There is enough of
unconsciousness
to liberate things from their history. And there
is enough of history to liberate unconsciousness
from its ascension.

-from "In Her Absence I Created Her Image" by
Mahmoud Darwish

Here's a story that might liberate your unconscious, because like you, your unconscious mind enjoys hearing stories about itself.

The Mind Sweepers

Floating in space are ancient particles (you might imagine them as beads of light or a kind of dust). These particles originated with the birth of the universe itself and they are charged with a particular magnetic energy, one that protects all cosmic and molecular systems against any major disruptions.

Somehow a huge number of these particles ends up being corralled into a mysterious capsule, probably by some destructive force trying to capture them and crash the whole system. One day, after floating in space for millions of years the capsule falls into the center of London where it is discovered by a young man who of course feels compelled to open it.

Because they are programmed to protect any organism they encounter, the ancient particles enter the man's blood stream and flow along until they come to a blockage in his energy system, caused by a core trauma lodged deep in his cellular memory: when he was a child, he had witnessed the death of his mother by an aerial bomb.

Recognizing that the man's deep desire to see his mother alive is causing him to suffer, the particles set out to help him find her. In other words, instead of allowing him to face the emotional truth of his mother's death, they cause him to act out his deepest desire in spite of the fact that it is irrational.

They program a script that he seems to have no control over and consequently his behaviors take on a life of their own. And you can imagine the horror show that this man's life becomes as he desperately seeks out his mother in every woman he meets. But the particles weren't trying to unleash mayhem—they were trying to fix things.

Sounds like a good storyline for an episode of Dr. Who, right? (And it is, although I took some creative license.)

But if you're reacting to things in a way you find perplexing, this scenario might sound familiar. We are all operating under basic programs that are habituated and when those programs run on auto-pilot we don't necessarily even know what the original trigger was, much less understand how these unconscious processes influence our conscious thoughts.

And there is something otherworldly about how, and why, our brains work this way. Because like the protective and ancient particles in the story, deep in your brain are two almond shaped masses of nuclei called *amygdala* that have stayed with us since the earliest days of our evolution as humans. (I love the word *amygdala*. It's a direct translation of the Arabic *al-lauzatan* which means, "the two almonds.") They are a part of our limbic system and are involved in processing the emotions that are related to survival — specifically fear, anger, and pleasure. They also are responsible for determining what memories are stored and where — which is why emotions and memory are usually intertwined.

In a way, the amygdala works like a protective shield and its job essentially is to magnify our fears. I know you must be thinking that a protective shield should be like a head-to-toe suit of armor—not a couple of almonds with projectile powers.

But if you think about it, the most powerful defense would be the one that protects you from danger by keeping what threatens you far, far away. Or, if you are in the midst of a dangerous situation, a powerful defense would respond before you have time to think, so that the punch you throw would come from a force you didn't know you had, or your legs would run with a speed you didn't know you were capable of.

Just think about what would happen if your amygdala were damaged and you didn't react at all when a horn from a fast moving vehicle blared in your ear. As Daniel Schacter writes in *Searching for Memory*, "the amygdala is perfectly positioned to evaluate the significance of incoming information, which is an essential function of emotion. Events of high significance require immediate attention and action; events of low significance can be safely ignored."

Isn't it really cool to know that you've got this almond control center handling all this for you?

Except (it's never that easy) the amygdala can't tell the difference between something that really happened, something you're seeing in a movie theater, and something you're experiencing in a dream.

Obviously the amygdala isn't trying to cause one over-reaction after another. It's trying to keep us alive.

So when you're watching a horror film and something appears out of the shadows and you freak out (meaning your heart rate elevates, you start to sweat, your blood rushes to your butt and causes you to almost jump out of your seat), your amygdala takes note. And every time you pass a shadow, every time you go to a lake, every time you walk alone down a quiet oak-lined lane in a sleepy suburb...

...you might feel afraid even if you're not exactly sure why. And this is because your amygdala has sensors that are protecting you, even when you consciously know that the situation is harmless. You might imagine these almond shaped knobs at the base of your skull as a sophisticated projection booth which responds to certain cues. In a flash it will fire off the memory of a trauma and cause you to freak out, even if the actual situation you've encountered doesn't warrant such an extreme response.

So if you seem to be over-reacting to every little thing, you might consider having a chat with almond control.

To say: hey, Amygdala. Everything is OK. My body is safe. I'm walking down this street, and I'm OK. You can reassure your brain that your body is safe by taking a few deep breaths and releasing them slowly. And smile because if you're breathing deeply and smiling, your brain is going to know that you're not in any danger. And breathe into that thought because the more you practice doing this on a daily basis the more your life will revolve not around swift and often irrational reactions, but rather your conscious awareness of yourself in time and space.

If possible, be present wherever you are by just noticing everything that you can see in your particular quiet reality at that moment.

And here's the most important thing about this: when you reassure your amygdala that you are not in danger...

when you are not walking around in a state of constant panic...

when you are present in your particular reality and are paying attention to what is actually there...

if ever you actually are threatened, you'll be ready and will respond in a heartbeat. And you will probably survive.

WHEN A BOX IS JUST A BOX

Of course this superimposition of memories, emotions, and bodily reactions doesn't have to be set off by something scary or traumatic — it could be something quite humorous. For example, I worked with a woman who felt she needed to control her portions. At the same time, she associated the refrigerator with an amazing sense of freedom — like she could do whatever she wanted because no one was "standing over" her. I thought her choice of words, "standing over me," was revealing a larger story and so I asked her to elaborate.

She recalled that when she was a kid her father was committed to teaching her and her siblings portion control. He would place a cereal box on top of the refrigerator in such a way that if she opened it when she wasn't supposed to, the box would fall on her head. Then her father would yell from the other room, "Who's that getting into the refrigerator?"

She was laughing as she told this story because she knew that her father wasn't trying to be mean. He was sincerely trying to teach his kids useful information about healthy eating. But somehow her amygdala and in turn, her unconscious mind registered this as a threat to her survival. So, to feel well nourished she eats too much and whenever she feels like it because no one is "standing over" her.

Was her unconscious mind conflating the sensation of hunger with the feeling of freedom for some other reason? I'm not a psychoanalyst and am not sure if it is always necessary or even possible to find the root cause of a particular issue.

I do know that if you're behaving automatically or reacting impulsively you can interrupt these patterns by introducing new information and different data. Because once your unconscious mind is made aware that its efforts are making things worse, it can correct things. It's on your side.

By laughing about this story and understanding that her father was well meaning in his intentions, she can work to no longer associate the refrigerator with the feeling of freedom. Instead, she can associate that feeling of freedom with things she wants to do in her life. She can build up her repository of inner resources which for her includes organizing her apartment, reading and writing, and taking long walks in the park with her son.

Lessons learned the hard way, repeated mistakes, and experiences that shape your reactions to things don't have to be relived over and over again in order for you to survive. And if you will believe this, you will also begin the work of bringing your conscious intentions into alignment with your unconscious reactions.

You road I enter upon and look around, I believe you are not all that is here,
I believe that much unseen is also here.

-from "Song of the Open Road" by Walt Whitman

YOUR OWN PRIVATE SPA

There is no doubt but that people really get into each other's business. Right now, there are people who are going out of their way to inflict psychological (and physical) warfare on their spouses. There are people who are playing power games to intentionally make other people feel inferior; people who are saying really messed up things to their kids (or not talking to them at all), causing them to feel threatened and insecure about the world.

And because it's impossible to imagine that injustice and violence are going to stop anytime soon, it's important that we build up (and teach) a repertory of coping skills. And that means becoming more self-aware than we've ever been, and adopting an internal language — a way of talking to ourselves — that our brains can rapidly learn and permanently retain.

But as anyone who has ever consciously tried to change a behavior knows, the lines of communication to our our own thought processes aren't always open.

Dr. John Sarno, author of *Healing Back Pain: The Mindbody Connection*, writes about how the mind&body connection sometimes seems to be controlled by forces that are beyond our conscious control. One of the great mysteries of evolution is why the human brain allows us to act out dysfunctional or even dangerous patterns (or endure chronic physical pain) rather than confront painful or scary emotions.

It's because our brain, a self-monitoring device evolved to keep us alive and safe, is always on the lookout for threatening emotions we are not prepared to confront consciously. When it encounters these "unprocessed" feelings (specifically fear and anger) our brain reroutes the associated emotional pain somewhere in the body — often in the lower back, stomach, or throat.

And people walk around with their lower backs burning, their stomachs churning, their throats and chests aching. They go to the doctor but nothing seems to be wrong.

And it's not as if consciously confronting repressed emotions is as easy as putting a few dollars in a photo booth and having the offending memory or sensation be revealed in an instant. There are layers upon layers of experiences, reactions, emotions, voices and self-talk that pile up; people who have the money and time to spend in therapy working through these layers can perhaps experience a kind of release.

Most people don't have this luxury, but are still looking for relief. Which is why so many of us seek out alternative therapies such as acupuncture, hypnosis, Reiki, and massage. And, in fact, these therapies can actually make sufferers like us feel better because for a couple days it can seem as if a weight has been lifted, or an inner space opened.

And for a couple hours after a good acupuncture or massage treatment (or a trip to the gym, a nice hike, a bike ride, or afternoon spent reading) you may walk around feeling more purposeful, like an arrow shot on a steady course in spite of the wind.

Maybe after a healing treatment you have a better perspective on a certain troubling situation. Maybe, for the time that the treatment is felt in your body, you're not so resentful of your job, or quite so stressed out by certain people in your life who seem to know all your hot spots. Instead, you're serene, calm, filled with a kind of steadiness that some people call inner peace. Walking a little more slowly, with a little more self-awareness. Feeling ok with the distractions, stressors, and uncertainties of the world.

Most of us know what this release is like, but most of us also find that after a day or two of inner serenity, the emotional weight comes back and the peaceful space closes. And then we go back to seeking any kind of treatment that will provide more lasting relief

If this cycle of temporary freedom from pain followed by a renewed search for a permanent "fix" is a pattern you've experienced, then then the good news is that you already know what it is to have "that feeling" of inner calm and balance.

And if you can conjure up "that feeling" (calm, relaxed, at peace, not over-reacting) then you'll also know what I mean when I say that eventually the feeling fades, and you go back to feeling just the way you did before the treatment, walk, vacation, etc.

But that's probably because you have an expectation that the treatment will heal you in some comprehensive way. Or, you believe that you can never really be healed because you attribute the power of "that feeling" to the therapist or healer, as if it has nothing to do with you.

But what if this isn't really true? What if "that feeling" is, right now, a memory that you are retaining somewhere in your body? And when you take a deep breath and think about that beach, yoga class, healing treatment, trip to the gym, you can feel (right now) a little calmer.

And instead of thinking that you need to seek out the perfect healer or stress-relieving treatment, you can begin to remember all the different times in your life when you felt this way. I don't know if you'll imagine swimming in the ocean or walking through the woods. Or if you'll imagine a hot stone massage or being in your bed when you are chilling out. You might imagine a meal that you made or that someone made for you, or the taste of peaches that first week in June when they are fresh.

Allow your mind to scan the files for "that feeling" and see what comes up. And you can know that these memories are resource states for you: a state of mind you can visualize in your mind and feel in your body. A state of mind, in other words, that allows you to breathe a little deeper.

Here's why this kind of creative thinking is important:

If you cultivate your ability to manifest "that feeling" you're doing a lot more than thinking positive thoughts. You're moving neural clusters from one area of the brain to another. Because the cells that fire together wire together, when you think the same thoughts over and over again you are creating a dynamic neural network called an "area of association." And that network can either work for you or against you depending on the thoughts.

According to Melissa Tiers, hypnotherapist and author of *The Anti-anxiety Toolkit: Rapid Techniques to Rewire Your Brain*, if your thinking results in psychological symptoms such as anxiety, "you can interrupt the anxiety and then connect that cluster to a more resourceful state like relaxation... [and] you will be cross connecting those neurons and loosening up the area of association that had been keeping that cluster strong."

So the next time you go to the gym, get a great massage, take a long walk, or hear an incredible concert don't just go through the motions of being there. Feel it. Breathe into it. Take it in like oxygen.

Because as you absorb it at this level, you will be somatically storing it in your body and mentally recording it in your mind so that in the future — when you're stressed out or dealing with something difficult in your life — you can call up this experience, which will have become "deeply wired" in your neural clusters. Always returning to you, even if unseen.

Feeling good in your life (and noticing how that feeling is anchored in your body) is not just about that moment. It's about future moments when you need to hit a reset button. When you're reacting to something in a way that doesn't feel good and you want to change your reaction as quickly as possible...

Stop. Take a breath. And see yourself in a place that is a resource state for you, feeling the way you want to feel.

And then book your week with as many opportunities as possible that will allow you to feel this way. Even if it's just during your lunch hour, or on your drive home from work.

I'm not saying that building up a slideshow of resource states is going to magically free you of physical and emotional pain overnight. But this change in your thinking will certainly encourage you to focus your mind on something other than the kind of life you no longer want to be living.

Better yet, all the other therapies you might be trying out will have a more lasting beneficial effect because instead of expecting one acupuncture session to cure you, you can ride the wave of how you feel after a session. You'll no longer be a piece of emotional driftwood; you'll be a surfer maneuvering through a tumultuous sea. Healing will happen from the inside, and get reinforced from the outside.

You've probably heard that idea before:

Peace comes from within. Do not seek it without.

- Buddah

But what will convince you that it's true?

The Motive for Metaphor

You like it under the trees in autumn,
Because everything is half dead.
The wind moves like a cripple among the leaves
And repeats words without meaning.

In the same way, you were happy in spring,
With the half colors of quarter-things,
The slightly brighter sky, the melting clouds,
The single bird, the obscure moon—

- from "The Motive for Metaphor" by Wallace
Stevens

You might notice that I am using a lot of metaphors to get these ideas (they're packages) across to you. And if anything about what I'm saying is coming through (they're radio signals), it's because at least a couple of these metaphors are (like water) sinking in.

If you listen to yourself talk, you'll begin to notice all of the different metaphors you use on a daily basis to communicate with other people. In fact, you're processing at least six metaphors per minute. Stephen Pinker, author of *The Stuff of Thought*, must be right when he says that people can't put words together without using allusions or allegories and that in attempting to communicate we reach for metaphors that remind us of the idea we're trying to convey. To think is to create a metaphor; metaphor is what connects abstract ideas to concrete experiences.

This technique is interesting because when it comes to having a meaningful conversation with your own brain it's important to know that metaphor is a key that will unlock your limbic system and the other important areas of your unconscious mindbody that you need to communicate with.

You know what anger feels like, for example. I wonder if you can think about a situation that makes you feel angry, and feel that way... now. Seriously, just try it. What pisses you off?

I must admit to getting pissed off at other drivers when they follow me too closely. I also hate it when I feel silenced by another person, or when I listen to certain politicians talking about everything they don't know.

And when I feel that feeling of inner rage I know I'm feeling it because _____ is happening in my body, and it feels like _____.

Because (for example) my body heat rises and I feel hot under the collar, brimming with rage. My eyes bulge out and my forehead frowns. My blood boils and I feel out of control.

The interesting thing about all of the metaphors that relate to anger is that they provide you with the strategy to get out of feeling that way. (But only if that feeling isn't doing any good by either protecting or defending you.)

If your blood is boiling, what needs to happen to that blood?

It needs to cool down.

If your eyes are bulging and the veins in your forehead are sticking out like a zombie's veins, what needs to happen to them?

They need to recede, smooth out.

And how about that quivering feeling, hands clenched, that signify you're out of control?

I need to calm down, get it out of my system.

And how do you do that?

I breathe, think about something else, close my eyes for a second, go out for a walk. Then I allow the rage to pass, and shake it off.

If you don't do something to cool the rage and get it out of your system, it will find its own way out and usually, that's not a good thing. It will be hard to avoid throwing that plate or swinging that punch. And certainly, that kind of physical reaction is one way of exorcising your ferocious anger-demon, but at a terrific price. Not only are you hurting yourself or another person, you're playing into that projection of yourself as being out of control. And you're firing off those neurons that will continue to keep that old, self-destructive network strong.

It might be interesting to notice that whatever you do in your daily life to manage or cope with anger (or anxiety, worry, disappointment) is either working, or not, at the level of metaphor.

So when you read that to think is to grasp a metaphor, and that metaphor is what connects abstract ideas to concrete experiences, you might begin to understand that this isn't just theory; it's how your mind and your body communicate with each other and create physiological reactions to mental thoughts and images. Which means that when you're confronted with undesirable emotions, you can use metaphor to lead yourself to a state of mind that feels better by thinking and feeling this simple mental dance that Melissa Tiers calls the "metaphoric two-step."

This feeling feels like a _____.

What needs to happen for _____ to feel better? (Or to dissipate, vanish, get in the back seat?)

The idea is that as you imagine this happening, you'll start to feel calmer. And when you're feeling like you have a little more perspective on the issue you can figure out how to take the first, smallest step to get out of that feeling and into a new one.

And having reached the summit
would like to stay there
even if the stairs are withdrawn

-from "The Blue Stairs" by Barbara Guest

BREAKING HABITS, BREAKING BREAD

Here's another way of thinking about the power of metaphor. We talk about "breaking habits" and say that for most people it takes 66 days for you to be convinced that a habit is gone for good. We talk about "releasing traumas" and say that it takes remembering the incident, but not feeling it in the same way (not collapsing, wilting, or breaking in the face of it) to be convinced that it is no longer running our emotional control room. We talk about "getting over" a person or event in our lives, and know we are successful when we think about that situation or person and no longer feel the pains of longing, or belonging, or regret.

As you now know, the words we use to describe these desires to "break," "release," and "get over" are themselves clues to how to do it. And the first step in this healing separation is to transform these words into visual images. The second step is to use your creative mind to elaborate on the story.

For example, if you are trying to "break a habit" imagine it as a scene in a cartoon world. What happens when a character breaks something?

I see a rock, and a character with huge hands who is crushing it; the pieces fly all over the place like confetti.

OR

I see a wall, and a character with a sledgehammer that is twice his size. He strikes the barrier at its weakest point, causing the wall to crumble.

And what happens next?

The confetti turns into a light, fluffy snow and covers the entire landscape.

AND

The character steps over the crumbled wall and into a field blooming with colorful wildflowers.

And when the character is in the field with the flowers, or in the landscape, what happens to the rock that was crushed, the wall that was smashed?

It's smaller. The rock has been reduced to a pile of pebbles; the wall is rubble and dust. They're fragments in a much bigger and more interesting field.

Perhaps you would like to try and compose your own little "metaphoric two-step" right now, by thinking about something that you would like to "get over."

Get over, like what? Imagine that wall, river, ocean, canyon (whatever it is) and think about what you would need to do to "get over" it. Imagine yourself doing just that, and take a moment to notice how imagining yourself bridging, flying, sailing feels in your body, right now. If you can feel a shift, even for a few moments, you've figured out how the mind and the body are one simultaneous and simpatico system, like waves and the deeper waters of the sea.

But of course you knew that already. You've blushed when someone made you feel embarrassed, bristled when someone told a bad joke. You've felt your heart pounding when you saw someone bleeding, and felt aroused at the sight of certain body parts.

You know that thinking can produce a feeling, and that feeling, if you really think about it, is exists somewhere in your body. Probably in the volatile area between your stomach and your throat.

Lingering, hovering, churning, wringing. Causing you to feel a certain way and quite possibly, causing you to react in response to how you are feeling.

So, what's happening in your body, right now?

And how does a body break
bread with the word when the word
has broken. Again. And. Again.
With the wine. And the loaf.
And the excellent glass
of the body. And she says,
Even. If. The. Sky. Is. Falling.
My. Peace. Rose. Is. In. Bloom.

-from "More Blues and the Abstract Truth" by C.D.
Wright

ख

I've seen several staged hypnosis
shows and they're always basically the
same. People doing silly or weird
things just because someone told them
to "sleep deeply NOW!" And certainly
there is a part of me that is thinking,
these people really believe that they
have been hypnotized to do these
things. And so they do these things.
That guy really does sound like he's
speaking Japanese and those two boys

really are moving their bodies like strippers.

But there's another part of me that also knows that these people who believe they are up there doing those things because some hypnotist told them to do those things are missing a tremendous opportunity.

If a showman can suggest that you are an opera singer and then suddenly without any training you sing the "Toreador Song" from *Carmen* without missing a note...

...imagine what you can do if YOU suggest to yourself that you can finish writing that novel, get that promotion, learn French, or achieve whatever you need in order to be the person you know yourself to be.

It's common to think that other people are controlling us. Or that our unconscious mind is running the show. Or that everything that is wrong in our lives is someone else's fault.

And who are we when we believe that?

Puppets on a string, victims of circumstance.

And what needs to happen to that puppet?

She needs to replace her strings with a bungee chord...

lineal
thought
backward
body

no one
knows
the brains
I am now

tree
an oar
origin

- from "...shift at oars" by Stacy Szymaszek

TRADING THOSE OLD BOOKS

One day several years ago my then three-year-old daughter tripped and fell on her cheek, banging it quite hard. A couple days after this incident, she started moving her head repetitively, a gesture that looked like she was trying to get the hair out of her eyes. But she kept doing it and soon the gesture was accompanied by her opening and closing her mouth. And then, she started opening and closing her hands, while doing all of the above.

We took her to a neurologist who wasn't concerned about any correlation between the fall and the tics. Rather, he felt that a child's brain is in such an active state of neurological wiring that it can easily get accidentally re-routed, thinking that it's doing the right thing, but actually getting confused. (Like a record playing the wrong track.) He also suggested that some people are more prone to tics than others, and that there is no cause for neurological concern unless the tics repeat non-stop for at least six months (in which case Tourette syndrome may be a possible diagnosis.)

She struggled with the tics on and off for five years, in varying levels of severity. For a while she couldn't stop doing the "thumbs up" gesture, and for a while she couldn't stop jumping. This tic was the worst of the lot because she was jumping all the time and it was tiring her out, but she couldn't stop. And when she started school, the other kids started making fun of her. One day when she was six we took a long walk with a friend to a playground that was a half hour away. On the way home, she couldn't stop jumping and kept on collapsing in frustration.

On that walk I worked with her to try and figure out the strategy behind those tics. She said that she heard a song in her head and had to jump at a certain part. So we tried singing a different song, and when that didn't work, jumping at a different place in the song. We made it back, but the effort was significant.

I read some research that linked tics to motion deficiency, and so we started bouncing. I have one of those bouncy Swedish ball chairs, and I would put her on it and we would bounce sixty times. I'm not sure if it helped the tics, but she certainly enjoyed the therapy and laughed the whole time.

As I write this, my daughter is now nine years old; in the last year it had become obvious to me that my daughter's tics have, at least for the moment, disappeared. I asked her about it, and this is what she said:

"I got rid of them."

"How did you do that?"

"I got rid of them cuz I had wanted to be like a grownup so I traded my tics in for becoming a child."

"So your tics were happening because you were trying to be someone else?"

"No, it's more like I traded a book for a different book."

I have no idea what she really means by this, and don't know how this idea of "trading" one thing for another came to her. And I'm not sure that any cause or effect is even the point of this story. She knows that something happened because she can feel the difference in how her body reacts. Whatever she did, she tapped into some deep part of herself and adjusted the information that was being processed there. And to describe the change, she had to think metaphorically.

So when you hear people talk about the power of metaphors and visualizations you can know that your imagination is not only about creativity. It's about the fact that your thoughts can and will produce alterations in your body's chemistry. This means that when you switch one metaphor for another one, you switch your perception of the problem and therefore switch your emotional response to it. Once that happens, the switches ignite a whole series of biochemical reactions that affect everything from your neural networks to your heart rate, your immune system to your genes. The metaphoric two-step is not just another waltz—it's the dance of your biochemistry as it reacts to fundamental shifts in your emotional state of mind.

A CLASSIC, REVISITED

Before you started reading this informative little book, you certainly knew on some level that your brain, ancient evolutionary miracle that it is, works behind the scenes of your conscious awareness to keep you alive, and even if it doesn't always respond to direct suggestions, it's still on your side. When we're behaving in a way that doesn't feel right, it can seem as if we're fighting a battle between conscious and unconscious forces. But there may be a more productive way of understanding this dialogue between different parts of our mind.

In fact, the American philosopher and psychologist William James didn't think that the term "unconscious" made any sense, because the prefix "un" seems to imply a negation of consciousness. Since it would be a paradox to think that consciousness could "un" itself, he preferred the term "co-conscious" and instead of dividing the conscious and unconscious forces, he saw them (metaphorically) as "two or more streams of thought proceeding simultaneously — one in awareness, others not."

I respond to that idea of the co-conscious mind, because it means that even if you occasionally slip into a thought-stream that is carrying you towards undesirable habits and patterns, your co-conscious mind can return you to the current of thought you'd rather be riding on. And one of the quickest ways to feel yourself moving between streams of thought is through your breath, which you can follow into thoughts and ideas that calm you down and give you insight.

To experience this you might want to try out a famous technique that comes from Richard Bandler and John Girder, the founders of a therapeutic model called NLP (Neuro Linguistic Programming). It's a useful technique for getting your conscious and co-conscious minds to collaborate: two streams intersecting and flowing together.

It begins with the acknowledgement that your mind and body are working together to keep you alive, and that at their core even the worst behaviors have a positive intention. This means that often when we get stuck repeating a certain pattern it is because that pattern makes us think that we are satisfying one (or more) of those core human needs we depend on to survive.

NLP coach Tony Robbins refers to what he calls the "six core needs," which he boils down to:

Certainty (security, comfort, safety)

Uncertainty (variety, adventure, challenge, rebellion)

Significance (recognition, pride, validation of who we are)

Connection (love, communication, feeling understood)

Contribution (giving back, leaving a mark on the world)

Growth (knowledge, learning, personal development)

So eating, for example, might make you feel full which at some level makes you feel taken care of. Smoking allows some people to feel rebellious and allows others to feel connected with other people. Some might associate "stuff" with safety, and so shopping can seem to be a powerful antidote when life gets difficult.

Obviously this kind of pop psychology doesn't account for the complexity of human behavior, but it's a useful exercise because when you think about that behavior you want to change, you might know right away what that positive intention is. And if you don't, just take a couple minutes to follow your breath and think about it.

You know how important your creative mind is (the one that allows you to transform metaphors and affect your biochemical state) so use it now to scan, as fast or as slow as you would like, your mental files. Ask yourself the question: what else can I do to satisfy that positive intention, that core human need?

As you search for alternatives to the unwanted behavior, don't be too hard on yourself. Some of these alternatives that occur to you may may seem silly or off-topic and others may be techniques that you have tried before without success.

Make a list and once you have an interesting range of options, go ahead and select a few that seem relevant to your life at this particular moment. Then use your creative mind to try each of these possibilities on – as if you are casting a movie and want to see how each actor will play out in a different role.

(You might also try on one of the silly or absurd ideas, being curious about why this idea came to you at this particular moment.)

Once you've decided on an approach, would you be willing to commit to this option for, let's say, a month? How about a week? Or even just two days?

And as you imagine yourself doing that thing to satisfy one of your core human needs for a couple of days...

...now see yourself taking the first smallest step that will initiate this process...

...the minute you get up from your chair.

And if you check in with yourself, and notice that all parts of you are in agreement, you can be sure that you have streamed your conscious and co-conscious minds into common waters. And what you can understand from this kind of convergence is that you are changing, and would like all of your minds to change with you. And as they do, you will find yourself reacting in new ways and behaving in new ways that are more in alignment with your overall goals and desires to become a fully functioning human being who acts and reacts not from a place of unconscious revolutions but a place of inner knowing.

Here's a summary of the exercise and it's a good one to practice when you need to get yourself back into alignment:

1) What positive intention is this behavior or situation serving in my life? Or, how is this behavior trying to serve me and protect me in some important way? (Keep in mind that denial, repression, self-medication, etc. emerge from positive intentions that can be

rewired or associated with something else.)

2) What alternative behaviors or thoughts would satisfy that positive intention in a better way? Come up with a list of both impossible (absurd, silly) options as well as obvious and practical ones.

3) Pick one or two alternative behaviors that you are willing to try out for a couple weeks, or even just a couple days. As you settle on these ideas, take a moment to imagine yourself doing them.

4) Notice how you're feeling in your body about this process. Is there any part of you that seems resistant to it? If so, become curious about that part of you. Turn it into a metaphor and move it around; ask yourself: what is the positive

intention behind this resistance? (And move through the questions again.)

ଔ

The more you practice this process the more the strategies you're learning in this book (and the ones you already knew) will teach you how to change the quality of the information you're presenting to that fascinating bodymind system of yours.

IT'S JUST A PLACEBO!

What I've come to understand about these strategies is that practicing them in the midst of stressful situations helps to neutralize the fear that the body is somehow in danger; and doing this, as far as I can tell from my own personal experience and research, is what activates the placebo effect.

The "placebo effect" used to be brushed aside in medical schools, but now research universities are starting to run double-blind tests to figure out how it works. And the results are not surprising. A recent UCLA study revealed that people who took a real pill and people who took a placebo both showed similar changes in brain activity. And a Harvard study revealed that symptoms of IBS decreased significantly even when participants were given a pill that they knew was a placebo.

Most people write about the connection between the placebo effect and belief – meaning that a patient's belief that a drug will or not work will become a self fulfilling prophecy. According to Dr. Bruce Lipton, author of The Biology of Belief, one-third of all healings — whether the cure comes from drugs, surgeries, or alternative treatments — are related to the perception of the patient. Which means that pleasing the patient by telling her: "35% of people who have this kind of disease survive" has got to be more beneficial to her than the dire diagnosis: "I'm sorry to tell you this, but you have a terminal disease." Given either diagnosis, her co-conscious mind is going to start processing the information. Knowing the effects that thoughts have on biochemistry, she may as well get a head start on believing that she just might survive.

Belief is certainly important. But I think the neutralization of fear also has a lot to do with the power of the placebo.

For example: There was a clinical study that was performed in Sweden in which volunteers were shown a series of anxiety-producing, unpleasant images (snakes, mutilated bodies, etc.). They were then given an anti-anxiety drug and told that it would reduce the negative emotions that they were feeling – and it did.

The next day the volunteers returned and the experiment was repeated. Only this time, the drugs that they were given were sugar pills. And yet, the results were comparable.

During the trail, the brains of the participants were scanned and revealed that when they took the placebo pill there was reduced activity in the emotional center of their brain – the part that controls our fight or flight response. This means that the placebo pill clearly neutralized the emotional fear that the amygdala magnifies when processing images that seem to threaten the person's safety.

> Far, near,
> the bivouacs of fear
> are solemn in the moon somewhere tonight,
> in turning time.
> -"DreamSong #61" by John Berryman

It's easy to find testimonials from people who have gone through surgery without anesthesia, or listen to women talk about what it's like to give birth without pain killers. As health insurance rates continue to rise and more and more people are stuck with less-than-adequate coverage, it's likely that alternative mental strategies will finally become mainstream—along with seemingly radical but ancient understandings about how our minds and our bodies work together to activate powerful internal healing resources.

As a medical dictionary defines it, the placebo is "a substance containing no medication and prescribed or given to reinforce a patient's expectation to get well." The roots of the word are traced back to the Latin verb "to please" and the term was first used medically in 1785: "a medicine given more to please than to benefit the patient."

But you don't have to see a doctor to start your own regimen of placebos. Once you know that the optimal state for changing an unwanted behavior or symptom is to neutralize your fear of it so that you can begin to take small action steps in ways that are more relaxed and therefore more conducive to your overall biochemistry, the healing process can begin to unfold in you.

I've studied medicine until I cried
All night. Through certain books, a truth unfolds.
Anatomy and physiology,
The tiny sensing organs of the tongue—
Each nameless cell contributing its needs.
It was fabulous, what the body told.

-from "What the Body Told" by Rafael Campo

Cultivate Your Placebos

For over twenty years my partner Richard had been unable to sleep through the night and for most of his life he had self-medicated a whole host of childhood traumas and adult overreactions with a daily dose of two martinis and several glasses of red wine. He was almost twenty pounds overweight when I met him five years ago and although he was doing all the right things—exercising, eating right, maintaining connections with his friends—he just couldn't lose it.

That all changed in one day. Well, sort of. We were traveling together in Amsterdam to present a breakout session at a conference.

On our first day there, Richard left his computer bag on the train platform. He had his passport in his coat, but his computer and all his notes were gone. The minute he realized this he took a moment to curse his negligence and then said something extraordinary to me.

He said, "I'm not going to let this ruin our trip. The universe has taken something away from me and the only way I'm going to get it back is to sacrifice something big in return. I'm going to stop drinking."

Although I was moved by his calm reaction to the situation, I wasn't sure I believed him. He had been drinking for over thirty years. But he did indeed quit, seemingly cold turkey, right there and then. And not surprisingly, a month later he was sleeping through the night and losing weight.

A few weeks after we returned, a letter arrived from the Amsterdam train authority. His backpack had been found and was on its way back to him. It arrived a few days later and of course the computer was gone. But inside was an envelope containing a smooth, five dollar bill. Was it his? Or did the person who took his computer leave it as some kind of exchange? We laughed when we saw it — the universe certainly has a strange sense of humor.

I asked him how he made this decision so abruptly. He said something that really stayed with me because it seems key to why I am writing this book:

I cultivated my placebos.

In other words, he didn't suddenly "just" stop drinking and start losing weight. Rather, he had been practicing small strategies over time, almost as if he had self-prescribed himself a series of placebos that reinforced his overall desire for change. Small steps, in other words, that laid down a track. And the more they were used, the easier the treading became.

For example, he had stopped eating processed foods and white flour; he started taking vitamins and running an extra kilometer in the gym. He was seeing an acupuncturist every other week and he had reconnected with his spiritual side by meditating more frequently. His life began to revolve around tending to these new behaviors, and without even knowing it consciously the positive intentions that used to be appeased by eating were starting to be replaced with other things that made him feel better.

At some point – call it the threshold, or the point of no return – it just didn't make sense for him to be cultivating those old behaviors any more. So at the moment when he left his backpack on the train platform the spark, match, and momentum were all in place to ignite a radical change. Because in cultivating small daily habits that made him feel good, he was in effect rewiring his brain to begin paying more attention to who he wanted to be than to who he no longer was. He prefers this new skin to the one he had been wearing and nothing – not even losing his computer – could make him turn back.

So you, right now. Sitting there on that chair, subway seat, or bed. You're revolving on solid ground. When your amygdala is calm and your placebos are allowed to bloom: that's where the journey to find all the resources you will ever need begins.

You, Returning...

At the beginning of the nineteenth century, Rabbi Nachman of Breslov read the Psalms of David and perceived in them the idea that within each of us are interior vibrations — like a frequency or pulse that, when harmonized, allow us to feel connected not only to ourselves but to the other living beings.

Describing this idea in his book *Mysteries of the Kabala* Marc-Alain Ouaknin writes, "If a person does not do this work of re-attachment through the intermediary of his thoughts by channeling them in the right direction, the resulting imbalance and unease may be translated into melancholy, depression, and illness."

A psychoanalyst might say that depression arises when a person's unconscious desires and drives (eg. to survive, to be loved) are on a different track from their conscious thoughts; that it is when the conscious and unconscious minds can be put into alignment that healing in a therapeutic sense can begin.

And Milton Erikson, the father of hypnotherapy puts it this way:

In everyday life one is continually confronted with difficult and puzzling situations that mildly shock and interrupt one's usual way of thinking. Ideally these problem situations will initiate a creative moment of reflection that may provide an opportunity for something new to emerge. Psychological problems develop when people do not permit the naturally changing circumstances of life to interrupt their old and no longer useful patterns of association & experience so that new solutions and attitudes may emerge .

-Milton Erikson from *Hypnotherapy: An Explanatory Casebook*

So what are the metaphors, visualizations, mental strategies, and other techniques you might imagine to usher in new solutions and attitudes? Or to articulate "that feeling" in your body when you are calm, not over-reacting, feeling the way you want to feel, and moving through your day in a way that makes you hopeful for more good days to come?

Some people describe this as being "attuned" (like a radio) to their higher power. Others might say that this feeling is like floating in calm water, or like sitting on a mighty rock that overlooks everything.

Others might say, "I just feel good. Like anything is possible. Like I can be who I want to be, like everything will be ok."

And the reality is that for most of us, this state of mind and body is not going to be accessible at every moment of every day. It's not as if once you feel it you can be completely immune to all the stresses and sufferings that life brings.

But once you feel it you can return to it. And it is in the ever-persistent process of returning that enlightenment (the earthly kind) just might happen.

Often I am permitted to return to a meadow
as if it were a scene made-up by the mind,
that is not mine, but is a made place,

that is mine, it is so near to the heart,
an eternal pasture folded in all thought
so that there is a hall therein

that is a made place, created by light
wherefrom the shadows that are forms fall.

- from "Often I Am Permitted To Return To A
Meadow" by Robert Duncan.

ACKNOWLEDGEMENTS

I'd like to thank Richard Ryan, Sophie Prevallet, Elaine Prevallet, Boyd Gilbert, Emily Skillings, and Martine Bellen for reading this manuscript and helping it to evolve through various stages.

My mentor and friend, Melissa Tiers, is the voice of practical wisdom and integral inspiration that sets the tone of this book.

For further reading:

Bandler, Richard and John Grinder. *Frogs Into Princes: Neuro-Linguistic Programming*. Real People Press, 1979.

Campo, Rafael. "What the Body Told" from *The World In Us: Lesbian and Gay Poetry of The Next Wave*. Stonewall Inn Editions, 2011.

Cortez, Jayne. "Neighbor" from *Somewhere In Advance of Nowhere*. High Risk Books, 1996.

Darwish, Mahmoud. "In Her Absence I Created Her Image" translated by Fady Joudah from *The Butterfly's Burden.* Copper Canyon Press, 2007.

Duncan, Robert. "Often I Am Permitted to Return to a Meadow" from *The Opening of the Field.* New Directions, 1960.

Erikson, Milton and Rossi, Ernest. *Hypnotherapy: An Exploratory Casebook.* Irvington Publishers 1979.

Guest, Barbara. "The Blue Stairs" from *The Collected Poems of Barbara Guest.* Wesleyan University Press, 2008.

Lipton, Bruce. *The Biology of Belief.* Hay House, 2008.

Moffat, Steven. "The Empty Child." *Dr Who* BBC Series 1, Episode 9. May 21, 2005.

Ouaknin, Marc-Alain. *Mysteries of the Kabala.* Abbeville Press, 2000.

Perlmutter, David and Villoldo, Alberto. *Power Up Your Brain: The Neuroscience of Enlightenment.* Hay House, 2011.

Placebos: "Placebos Work: Even Without Deception" in *Harvard Gazette*, March 31, 2012 and "Belief in Placebo Produces Physical Changes in the Brain, UCLA Study Reveals" in *UCLA News*, February 17, 2004.

Pinker, Stephen. *The Stuff of Thought: Language as a Window into Human Nature.* Penguin Books, 2007.

Rexroth, Kenneth. "The Wheel Revolves" from *The Collected Shorter Poems*, New Directions, 1966.

Roberson, Ed. "At the Far Edge of Circling" from *To See the Earth Before the End of the World*, Wesleyan University Press, 2010.

Sarno, John. *The Mindbody Prescription: Healing the Body, Healing the Pain.* Warner Books, 1998.

Schacter, Daniel. "The Brain's Almond: Amygdala, Emotion, and Memory" in *Searching for Memory: The Brain, the Mind, and the Past*. Basic Books, 1996, (212-217).

Siegel, Dan. *Mindsight: The New Science of Personal Transformation*. Bantam Books, 2010.

Stevens, Wallace. "The Motive for Metaphor" from *The Palm at the End of the Mind*. Vintage Books, 1971.

Szymaszek, Stacy., ". . . shift at oars" from *Emptied of All Ships*. Litmus Press, 2005.

Tiers, Melissa. *The Anti-Anxiety Toolkit* and *Integrative Hypnosis: A Comprehensive Course in Change*. Center for Integrative Hypnosis, 2011.

Whitman, Walt. "Song of the Open Road." http://www.poetryfoundation.org/poem/178711

Wright, C.D. "More Blues and the Abstract Truth" from *Steal Away: New and Selected Poems. Copper Canyon,* 2002.

Kristin Prevallet is a consulting hypnotist certified through the National Guild of Hypnotists and an Integral Life Coach certified through the International Association of Counselors and Therapists. She received a M.A. in Humanities through the University of Buffalo and has received residencies and awards from the New York Foundation for the Arts, PEN America, the Poetry Society of America, George Mason University, and Spalding University. A visiting professor at Eugene Lang College, she currently directs the Center for Mindbody Studies where she leads workshops and works with private clients. Her writings on poetics and consciousness have appeared in a variety of publications including *Spoon River Review*, *The Chicago Review*, *Fourth Genre*, and *Reality Sandwich*; she is the author of four books including *I, Afterlife: Essay in Mourning Time* and most recently, *Everywhere Here and in Brooklyn: A Four Quartets*. She frequently writes about hypnosis and mental strategies on www.trancepoetics.com.

Many thanks for reading this book. Send feedback and responses to kristin@mindbodystudies.com and if you're interested in reading more of my writings or hearing about exciting new products, please consider joining my mailing list at www.mindbodystudies.com.

More in the Creative Rewiring Series
available online at
www.mindbodystudies.com

Two guided recordings composed by Kristin
Prevallet with a soundscape by Ambrose Bye

Sleep (wide reality)

A 50 minute mp3 designed to lead you into a comfortable sleep.

Automatic Writing (release your writing mind)

A 23 minute mp3 designed to release your unconscious mind through writing.